CW01512638

Original title:
Ruddy Quills Across the Witch Hook

Author: Daisy Dewi
ISBN HARDBACK: 978-1-80563-182-8
ISBN PAPERBACK: 978-1-80564-703-4

The Veil of Night's Feathered Muse

In the stillness where shadows weave,
A whispering breeze takes flight,
With feathers soft, like dreams they cleave,
To paint the canvas of the night.

Beneath the stars, their secrets soar,
Each twinkle holds a tale untold,
Of ancient tales from times of yore,
In silver threads, the moonlight's gold.

A song is sung by nightingales,
Their notes like raindrops on the dew,
With every note, a story trails,
Entwined with whispers meant for few.

The veil of night, a shroud divine,
Wrought with magic, soft and fine,
The feathered muse, a guide so true,
Awakens dreams in hearts anew.

Quicksilver Shadows and Scarlet Stories

In alleyways where secrets hide,
Live fleeting glances, soft and sly,
With quicksilver shadows, dreams abide,
Where scarlet stories weave and fly.

A flickering flame in dusk's embrace,
Illuminates the paths we tread,
With every step, a twist of fate,
In whispered tales, the brave are led.

Beneath the moon's watchful gaze,
Heroes rise and battles fade,
In tapestries of crimson haze,
We find our strength, our fears allayed.

The pen, it dances with delight,
As shadows swirl in wild ballet,
Each stroke ignites the starry night,
And brings our dreams to light each day.

The Witch's Enchanted Pen

In a cottage draped in ivy's charm,
A witch sits with her quill in hand,
She conjures spells to shield from harm,
With ink that flows like silver sand.

Her parchment holds the fates of kings,
And whispers secrets of the lost,
With every sweep, her spirit sings,
Of love and magic, worth the cost.

A flick of wrist, a heartfelt line,
Transforms the mundane into the rare,
In every word a thread divine,
That weaves the fabric of the air.

The witch, she knows what hearts desire,
With naught but ink and a fervent breath,
Her pen ignites a dormant fire,
Awakening life, beyond mere death.

In the Realm of Fetters and Quills

In boundless realms where echoes roam,
Where fetters break and spirits sing,
With quills in hand, we find our home,
In stories birthed from magic's wing.

Each word a key to hidden doors,
That lead us to the worlds unknown,
Beyond the sea, on distant shores,
Where every dream is freely sown.

The air alive with tales unspun,
Awaits the touch of fervent minds,
Beneath the blazing summer sun,
In every heart, a tale that binds.

So take your quill, and write with zeal,
Unshackle thoughts that yearn to soar,
In realms where we can truly feel,
The magic of forevermore.

Blood-Red Ink and Whispered Incantations

In shadows deep where secrets dwell,
A quill of night writes tales to tell.
With each stroke soft, the whispers flow,
Of ancient spells and the seeds they sow.

Beneath the moon's pale, ghostly light,
The words ignite, taking to flight.
With crimson ink that stains the page,
A witch's heart unleashed her rage.

Through tangled woods where cauldrons brew,
The echoes rise, a chilling crew.
Each letter sighs with dreams forlorn,
In blood-red ink, a curse is born.

Mystic voices weave their dance,
Entwining fate in a dark romance.
With every charm, the power grows,
In whispered paths, the magic flows.

So gather round, both kin and foe,
And heed the tales the shadows know.
For in this ink, the truths are masked,
In whispered spells, the past is tasked.

Feathered Secrets in the Foggy Hollow

In foggy hollows, whispers glide,
With feathered secrets, dreams abide.
The owls take flight on silent wings,
To share the tales the night time sings.

Among the shadows, creatures loom,
Beneath the veil, the mysteries bloom.
A flick of tail, a rustling leaf,
In moonlit paths, we find belief.

Each feather dropped tells stories old,
Of ancient lore in twilight's hold.
The woodland folk with twinkling eyes,
Guard treasures wrapped in softest sighs.

With every gust, the secrets swirl,
As magic spins and fates unfurl.
The fog would tease and beckon near,
To grant the bold their heart's true cheer.

So venture forth, be brave and wise,
In feathered whispers, truth defies.
For in the depths where shadows play,
The hollow keeps what night can't sway.

The Witch's Script of Forgotten Legends

Upon the parchment, aged and worn,
The witch's script, by moonlight sworn.
In looped and curling letters, dreams,
Unfurling tales of magic's themes.

With careful hands, the words ignite,
In every line, a spark of light.
Forgotten legends, fierce and bold,
In whispers passed, their truths unfold.

The cauldron's steam, like velvet air,
Conceals the fables, rich and rare.
Each potion penned, a vivid glimpse,
Of realms unseen, of mystic hymns.

Beneath the stars where shadows creep,
These scripts invite the brave to leap.
For every tale that's etched in time,
Holds hidden worlds that softly chime.

So let the witch's ink take flight,
In swirling forms through endless night.
For written spells will find their way,
And breathe to life what dreams convey.

Crimson Canvases of the Witching Hour

When twilight spills its crimson hue,
The witching hour comes into view.
On canvases where shadows meet,
A tapestry of bonds is sweet.

With each stroke bold, the colors dance,
As magic swirls in fateful chance.
The night unveils its hidden art,
A painter's heart knows where to start.

In swirling mists, the portraits speak,
Of whispered dreams and magic's peak.
Each brush of fate, a tale confined,
In shades of crimson, truth entwined.

Beneath the stars, the night does sigh,
As echoes weave, they gently fly.
For every canvas tells a tale,
Of witches bold who dared to sail.

So linger where the colors glow,
Amidst the tales of ebb and flow.
For in the hour of fading light,
The witching dance takes cheerful flight.

Scarlet Visions at Dusk's Edge

In twilight's grasp, the shadows creep,
A canvas brushed in shades of deep.
Scarlet whispers fill the air,
As dreams and secrets find their pair.

The stars awaken, one by one,
A tapestry of night begun.
Crimson hues in fading light,
Enshrine the magic of the night.

With every heartbeat, shadows play,
As dusk transforms the end of day.
A soft enchantment lingers near,
As twilight dances, crystal clear.

In whispers low, the secrets call,
Painting tales upon the wall.
The dusk holds visions, vibrant, bright,
The scarlet dreams take wondrous flight.

So linger here, in twilight's lace,
Where colors merge and glimmers grace.
In every shadow, find a sign,
The edge of dusk, where stars align.

Whispers of a Darkened Sky

Beneath the cloak of midnight's thread,
The secrets of the night are spread.
A haunting call, a gentle sigh,
Whispers echo in the sky.

With every star, a story told,
Of battles fought and dreams of gold.
The moonlight drapes, a silver sheet,
Where shadows linger, soft and sweet.

In silence deep, the world holds breath,
The night unfolds, a dance with death.
Yet beauty blooms in darkest shade,
Where quiet longings are not frayed.

With whispers soft, the night reveals,
The hidden truths that darkness steals.
In shadowed corners, visions stay,
Alive in whispers, night to day.

So heed the call, the darkened skies,
Where secrets dwell and magic lies.
In twilight's glow, seek all that's rare,
For whispers of the night declare.

Ink-Stained Feathers of the Night

Beneath the moon's translucent glow,
Ink-stained feathers dance and flow.
Their tales are etched in starlit streams,
A tapestry of woven dreams.

Each feather holds a story vast,
Of glorious futures and shadowed pasts.
They flutter forth, like spirit's flight,
In echoes fading with the night.

A million voices softly blend,
Where night and ink eternally tend.
With whispered truths, they draw us near,
An artful dance of joy and fear.

As twilight deepens, shadows loom,
A chorus rises from the gloom.
Ink-stained feathers, rich and wise,
Reveal the magic 'neath the skies.

So gather round, let stories spill,
In ink-stained dreams, hearts dare to thrill.
For every feather's gentle sweep,
Holds secrets of the night, to keep.

A Dance of Crimson Feathers

In twilight's glow, the sketches weave,
Crimson feathers take their leave.
They swirl around in wild delight,
A dance that spans the boundless night.

With every twirl, a tale takes shape,
Of dreams that rise and hands that drape.
In shadows cast by moonlit streams,
Crimson visions stir our dreams.

The night invites, a soft embrace,
A dance unfolds in timeless space.
As whispers float on fragrant air,
Crimson feathers, light as care.

With every heartbeat, rhythm flows,
A melody that gently grows.
In every step, a spark ignites,
The dance transcends mere summer nights.

So join the waltz beneath the sky,
Where crimson feathers twirl and fly.
In music soft, and magic spun,
The dance of night has just begun.

Blood-Winged Words in Dusk's Embrace

In twilight's clutch, whispers flow,
With blood-winged words, secrets grow.
The shadows dance, wild and free,
As dusk entraps the heart of me.

Beneath the boughs where silence hums,
A melody of fate succumbs.
Ink stains the night, poised to sing,
Of dreams that haunt a sheltered wing.

Fires flicker, tales untold,
With every sigh, the past unfolds.
Ink and paper bound in fate,
Awaits the heart, the whispered wait.

In corners dim, the worlds collide,
As shadows wrap the hearth's warm tide.
With every turn, the clock's soft beat,
Time trails like ghosts beneath our feet.

So let us wade through evening's grace,
With ink-stained hands, our dreams embrace.
For in this realm where dusk is king,
Blood-winged words shall rise and sing.

Luminescent Shadows on Dark Pages

In ink-encrusted realms of night,
Luminescence dances bright.
Shadows whisper, dark yet clear,
Stories penned with hope and fear.

On pages worn, the truth entwined,
With every stroke, a thread defined.
Ghostly figures softly glide,
Between the lines where dreams abide.

The quill becomes the wand of fate,
Casting spells that slowly satiate.
Through winding tales and haunted prose,
The heart of silence gently grows.

Ink spills forth like autumn's breeze,
With every flick, the mind's at ease.
We wander realms of whispered lore,
Where light and dark forever soar.

In every tale, a spark ignites,
A battle 'twixt the days and nights.
On darkened pages, truth emerges,
As luminescent shadow surges.

Quills Behind the Veil of Night

Within the veil where silence keeps,
Quills pen thoughts while the world sleeps.
In shadows deep, the stories sigh,
A tapestry of tales that fly.

With every stroke, a dream takes wing,
Under the moon's soft, tender ring.
The quill's caress, a lover's touch,
Unveils the night, reveals so much.

With ink that flows like rivers wide,
The heart unfolds, no need to hide.
Echoes whisper through the air,
Casting spells of hope and care.

The stars align with every word,
In the stillness, a voice is heard.
A symphony of thoughts collide,
With the quill as our guide and pride.

Beneath the shroud of starlit skies,
The words take flight, they soar and rise.
Through realms unseen, we find the light,
With quills behind the veil of night.

Shadowed Glyphs by the Mystic Waters

In whispered tides, the glyphs unfold,
Their secrets held in currents bold.
A dance of shadows, soft and low,
A tale of magic in the flow.

Beneath the stars, the waters gleam,
Where dreams are spun from silver seam.
In every ripple, a story sways,
Of ancient nights and misty ways.

The moonlight casts a shimmering shade,
On quiet shores where wishes played.
The air is sweet with hope's embrace,
In this enchanted, tranquil space.

Where silence speaks, and hearts are bared,
The echoes of the past are shared.
As shadows stretch and twilight sighs,
The whispers lift to starry skies.

Ember-Tipped Pens and Ancient Spells

With ember tips, the quills ignite,
In candle's glow, they weave the night.
Each stroke a spark, of art and lore,
Unlocking worlds from pages' core.

The ink flows deep, like rivers wide,
In scripts where secrets dare to hide.
From parchment old, the spells arise,
In woven tales, the magic lies.

Through whispered words, the visions gleam,
As fire dances with the dream.
A story penned in twilight's breath,
Of life and love, of hope and death.

With every line, a fate is drawn,
In shadows cast by silver dawn.
The pages turn, the heartbeats race,
In every tale, a timeless grace.

The Scarlet Script of the Night Sorceress

In scarlet ink, the sorceress writes,
A tapestry spun of starry nights.
Her quill, a wand in hands so deft,
With every stroke, a spell is heft.

The moon above, a guardian bright,
Watches over her sacred rite.
The air is thick with whispered dreams,
As magic flows in vibrant streams.

Beneath the cloak of twilight's veil,
Her flickering thoughts begin to sail.
Through shadows deep, the stories weave,
In every heart, a chance to believe.

The parchment burns with tales untold,
Of love and loss, of brave and bold.
Each verse reveals a hidden tryst,
In every letter, a precious twist.

Inked Secrets of the Enchanted Forest

In the heart of woods so deep and wide,
Where secrets in the shadows bide,
The trees whisper tales of old,
In inked whispers, their truths unfold.

The forest hums a quiet tune,
Beneath the watchful, silver moon.
With every breeze, the branches sway,
A velvet night, the spirits play.

In hidden glades, the magic brews,
With whispered names and ancient news.
Each leaf a page, each stone a word,
In every sigh, the soul is stirred.

As shadows lengthen and dreams arise,
The forest sheds its earthly guise.
With inked secrets, it gently calls,
A world where faded memory falls.

Quills of Fire and Darkened Dreams

In the quiet of the dim-lit room,
Quills dance like flames in the gloom.
Each stroke a whisper of secrets untold,
Crafting spellbound visions, vibrant and bold.

Shadows flicker, the candles sway,
As ink flows freely, dreams come to play.
A tapestry woven with wishes and fears,
Maps of emotion, born from our tears.

With every movement, a tale unfurls,
In the heart of the night, as magic twirls.
Hearts beat faster, the narrative spins,
In the web of stories, where courage begins.

Beneath the stars, the words ignite,
Chasing the darkness, embracing the light.
Quills of fire in the hands of fate,
Writing the future, we shall not wait.

In the morning glow, the ink shall dry,
Another chapter, as time passes by.
So take your quill, let your dreams soar,
For in darkened tales, there's always more.

Spellbound Tales on Scarred Pages

Pages weathered, with stories worn,
Each word a relic, through magic reborn.
Spellbound tales on scarred pages lie,
Whispering secrets that never die.

In twilight's embrace, old legends call,
Echoing softly in the shadowy hall.
Where heroes once triumphed, now ghosts take flight,
Fables entwined with the fabric of night.

With quill in hand, the scribe takes aim,
To weave a story that stirs like a flame.
Yet caution must guide the ink that flows,
For power resides in the tale one knows.

In the heart of a tome, treasure awaits,
Unlocking the magic which every soul gravitates.
And when the dawn breaks, these pages will glow,
With the spark of creation, a radiant show.

So linger a while, in this world of dreams,
Where the ink spills softly, and magic redeems.
In every scar, a journey, a sign,
For every story is yours, and mine.

The Forbidden Ink of the Night

In the depths of the night, shadows conspire,
A cauldron of secrets, swelling with fire.
Forbidden ink flows with power unseen,
Crafting desires where darkness once reigned.

With quills dipped in starlight, we write our fate,
On parchment untouched, where dreams resonate.
Each stroke a venture into realms unknown,
In the forbidden dance, we find our own.

The silence whispers of magic profound,
Echoes of caution in each mystic sound.
For those who dare peek beyond the veil,
Shall find both enchantment and shadows that trail.

Beneath the moon's gaze, a spark ignites,
Ink of the night, where destiny writes.
Stories of valor, twisted with strife,
Flames of ambition breathe life to this life.

So take heed, dear scribe, in the still of the dark,
With each drop of ink, you're leaving a mark.
In the pages unwritten, so much to explore,
For the forbidden calls; will you open the door?

Wandering Words and Feathered Ink

Wandering words through the pages roam,
With feathered quills, they seek a home.
Every letter a journey, a sight to behold,
In the warmth of the firelight, stories unfold.

Across the landscape of dreams we tread,
With ink, our compass, where imagination is fed.
Each tale a treasure, a magic spun thread,
Weaving lives together with words that are said.

Underneath the sky, with stars as guides,
Whispers of wonder where adventure abides.
In valleys of thought, where silence is know,
The pen takes flight, allowing hearts to grow.

Through realms of the fanciful, we drift and glide,
With feathered ink, wander side by side.
For in every heart, a story awaits,
To be penned with passion, unfurling the gates.

So let us embark on this quest we adore,
With wandering words, we forever explore.
In a world of adventure, magic, and hue,
With feathered ink, we'll write our debut.

In the Company of Scarlet Dreams

In twilight's dance, where shadows play,
Scarlet dreams whisper, drift away.
To realms unseen, our spirits soar,
While hearts entwine on fate's soft shore.

Amongst the whispers of the night,
We chase the echoes, take to flight.
A tapestry woven with hopes and schemes,
In the gentle fold of scarlet dreams.

The world retreats, the stars ignite,
Each flicker tells of truth and light.
In every pulse of pulse we share,
The starlit path leads us somewhere rare.

With laughter weaving through the air,
We find a magic, pure and rare.
In friendship's glow, fears shed their seams,
As we dance together in scarlet dreams.

And when dawn breaks, with colors bright,
We'll carry forth that tender light.
For in our hearts, forever gleams,
The endless grace of scarlet dreams.

The Winged Secrets Beneath the Moon

Beneath the moon, where shadows creep,
Winged secrets stir from silent sleep.
On silken threads, they softly glide,
In whispered tones, our truths confide.

Feathers brush against the night,
With every beat, a spark ignites.
We chase the dreams that take to flight,
In the gentle glow of fading light.

The stars above sing tales concealed,
In soft embraces, our fate revealed.
Through winding paths of moonlit streams,
We find our way to hidden dreams.

A bond unbroken, spirits free,
Together we unlock the mystery.
With every whisper, we grow bold,
In the stories that the night unfolds.

Through realms of wonder, side by side,
The secrets dwell where dreams abide.
In harmony, we navigate the trails,
With winged secrets, our hearts set sails.

Twilight Quills and Enchanted Ink

With twilight quills, our stories flow,
In enchanted ink, we let them glow.
Each word a spell, each line a song,
Through pages worn, we travel long.

The ink reveals what hearts conceal,
In every verse, the dreams we feel.
We write of love, of loss and fight,
In twilight's glow, we craft the light.

In whispered tales of yesteryears,
The laughter shared and hidden tears.
Together weaving realms so grand,
With every stroke, we take our stand.

The echoes linger in the air,
With every quill, a wish laid bare.
Each chapter holds a piece of us,
In twilight's grace, we learn to trust.

When ink runs dry and pages turn,
Our stories live, forever burn.
In twilight's embrace, we'll never sink,
For we create in enchanted ink.

A Journey Through Feathered Nightmares

In shadows deep, where whispers loom,
Feathered nightmares stir in gloom.
With every flutter, fears take flight,
A journey starts beneath the night.

Through winding paths of dark and light,
We face the phantoms born of fright.
Yet courage blooms in midnight's heart,
With every step, we play our part.

The skies awaken, restless skies,
As hidden truths slip past our eyes.
In dreams distorted, we find the way,
To turn the dark into the day.

With feathered wings, we learn to soar,
To face the dreams we can't ignore.
In the dance of fear, grace prevails,
Through feathered nightmares, hope unveils.

As dawn approaches, shadows flee,
Our hearts embrace the wild and free.
With wisdom gained, we're bold and bright,
A journey crowned in morning light.

The Allure of Mysterious Feathers

In the hush of twilight's glow,
Feathers drift where whispers flow.
Each hue a hint of secrets spun,
In shadows where the lost have run.

Glistening soft in silken air,
They beckon stories, faintly bare.
A soft breeze carries their sweet song,
Of wanderers where they belong.

In forests deep, on moonlit stage,
Nature's quills, a timeless page.
A dance of dreams with every flight,
Breathless beneath the starry night.

Hidden paths those feathers weave,
Tales of joy, of hearts that cleave.
In every plume, a life resides,
In each, the beauty of hidden tides.

So as you stroll, let spirits guide,
Follow where the shadows hide.
In every shimmer, a clue to find,
The allure that calls the heart and mind.

Enchanted Scripts in a Night's Embrace

Underneath the pale moon's light,
Scripts of silver take their flight.
Words that shimmer, dance, and bend,
In whispers, tales of dreams extend.

With quills of stars, they etch the sky,
Songs of ages drifting by.
A parchment sky, both vast and deep,
Holds secrets that the shadows keep.

Lines of fate in breezes swirl,
Casting spells that softly curl.
Each letter drips with lore so bright,
Crafted in the gentle night.

Beneath the trees, they softly sigh,
Echoes of a time gone by.
In every stroke, a heartbeat flows,
A story waiting to be chose.

So gather close, and let them teach,
The wonders that the night can reach.
In ink of dreams, the world expands,
With enchanted scripts in gentle hands.

Whirlwind Stories of the Witch's Spire

In twilight's grace, the tower stands,
Whispers beckon with bony hands.
A witch resides within its stone,
Guarding tales of the unknown.

Her cauldron bubbles, secrets stir,
A whirlwind where the shadows purr.
In every flicker of the flame,
Lies a haunting, whispered name.

Ancient lore in the air does creep,
As night unfolds, the stories leap.
With each enchantment, echoes soar,
Through misty dreams on hidden shores.

Vivid visions dance and play,
Unraveling history's sway.
In the spire where the spirits sigh,
The tales of old refuse to die.

So venture forth, let magic guide,
To where the witch's heart resides.
For in her world, the moments blend,
Whirlwind stories that never end.

Scarlet Hues of the Enchanted Night

When evening drapes its scarlet veil,
Magic stirs, a gentle trail.
In shadows rich with whispered dreams,
The night unfolds in vibrant schemes.

Crimson hues and splashes bright,
Of starlit dances in the night.
In every corner, secrets glow,
A symphony that winds and flows.

With every rustle through the trees,
The air is thick with whispered pleas.
A nightingale in shadows sings,
Of love and hope, of wondrous things.

The silver moon, a watchful eye,
Watches as the shadows lie.
In scarlet hues, the world ignites,
Bearing witness to the flights.

So linger long, beneath the spell,
In scarlet shades where dreams compel.
For night unfolds in colors bright,
A tapestry of pure delight.

Crimson Feathers Beneath the Crescent Moon

In the night's embrace, whispers take flight,
Crimson feathers dance, a magical sight.
Beneath the crescent, secrets softly hum,
A world of wonder, where night creatures come.

Stars light the path, shadows intertwine,
Ancient tales linger, under moon's gentle shine.
With each little flutter, the dreams come alive,
In silence they weave, where the lost spirits thrive.

Echoes of laughter, carried by the breeze,
Rustling of leaves, as time seems to freeze.
A flicker of magic, sparking the air,
As the world turns enchanted, beyond all compare.

Glistening dew drops adorn the dark clay,
Whispers of histories, they softly convey.
In this hidden realm, secrets unfold,
As crimson feathers shimmer, priceless and bold.

So linger awhile, beneath the crescent's glow,
Join the immortal dance, let your spirit flow.
For in this moment, all wishes take flight,
In the heart of the night, everything feels right.

Enchanted Ink and Twilight Whispers

In twilight's embrace, secrets spill like ink,
Stories entwined, giving hearts time to think.
Pages are turning, the magic ignites,
Words softly dripping, like shimmering lights.

The quill finds its rhythm, a dance in the dark,
As shadows around weave a spell, a spark.
Enchanted ink flows, tales yearn to be spun,
With each whispered sigh, a new journey begun.

From depths of the night, dreams take to the sky,
Bound in the pages, where fears dare to fly.
Twilight whispers secrets, secrets of old,
Upon fragile parchment, mysteries unfold.

So pick up the quill, let your spirit take flight,
In the realm of the ink, there's magic each night.
A world waits to bloom, with every soft touch,
Enchanted ink flows, awakening so much.

Amidst the shadows, where silence confides,
Stories awaken, like the moonlight that hides.
In twilight's embrace, let your heart gently dance,
With enchanted ink, seize this wondrous chance.

Scarlet Scribbles on Forbidden Scrolls

On ancient scrolls, where secrets reside,
Scarlet scribbles hide, as ambitions collide.
Whispers of power in symbols and signs,
Written in shadows, where dark magic twines.

Forbidden to touch, yet yearning to know,
Knowledge enchained, in its crimson glow.
Each line holds a story, a truth to unfold,
In this perilous dance, where the brave turn bold.

Curiosity brews, like potions in flames,
Voices from legends, calling out names.
Histories linger, like ghosts in the night,
Entwined in the words, shrouded in fright.

So delve into magic, with heart and with care,
For the scribbles they bear, are something rare.
Caught in temptation, the pages allure,
In scarlet's embrace lies the perilous cure.

Who dares to uncover the tales that are sworn?
From the shadows of night, new destinies are born.
With every stroke made, the universe bends,
In scarlet scribbles, the journey transcends.

The Witch's Pen in the Gloomy Grove

In a grove steeped in shadows, where secrets seem shy,
The witch's pen whispers, a soft lullaby.
With ink of the night, she conjures and spins,
A tapestry woven where magic begins.

Gloom wraps the trees, hiding stories untold,
Each stroke of her pen brings the brave and the bold.
As twilight deepens, her visions take flight,
In the heart of the woods, where the moon shines bright.

Her parchment a portal, each page a new world,
Where dreams intertwine, and fate is unfurled.
From shadows arise, creatures long since forgot,
In the witch's embrace, all fears turn to naught.

With whispers of wisdom, she guides the lost souls,
In the gloomy grove, where the night gently rolls.
Her pen filled with magic, she shifts time and space,
Etching in silence, her own secret grace.

So wander in wonder, let the stories ignite,
In the witch's domain, where darkness meets light.
For within every line, there's a spark to behold,
In the art of the witch, the universe unfolds.

The Witch's Quill: A Dark Romance

In shadows deep, where secrets dwell,
A witch sat crafting tales to tell.
Her quill dipped in ink of night,
Wrote of love, both dark and bright.

With every stroke, a heart would bleed,
Enchantments spun, a haunting creed.
Love entwined with bitter doom,
In velvet whispers, shadows loom.

The moonlight kissed her silver page,
A trap for souls, a gilded cage.
Through tempest winds, her laughter soared,
Yet in her heart, a pain stored.

A tragedy, her twisted song,
In every verse, where dreams went wrong.
She penned the fate of those lost before,
An endless cycle, forevermore.

The ink ran dry, yet still she wrote,
Of tender glances and love's cruel boat.
In candle's glow, her tears would fall,
For every heart, she loved them all.

Ethereal Wings at Dusk's End

Beneath the sky where twilight glows,
Ethereal wings in shadows rose.
A dance of light as day does bow,
To starry nights, eternal vow.

With whispers soft, the breezes sigh,
As dreams take flight, like birds they fly.
In silken hues, the dusk entwines,
A tapestry where magic shines.

The stars begin their radiant play,
Guiding weary souls astray.
With every beat, a promise swells,
In every heart, a story dwells.

The twilight shades a world anew,
Where hopes and wishes twirl and skew.
Beneath the veil of whispered light,
Ethereal wings fade into night.

At dusk's end, a truth unfolds,
In starlit dreams, the brave and bold.
With every breath, the magic flows,
As night unveils what daylight chose.

Whispering Shadows on Feathered Wings

In the quiet woods, where shadows creep,
Whispering secrets, the night does keep.
Feathered wings brush the cooling air,
A chorus of dreams sings everywhere.

By silvery streams, the spirits glide,
Where hopes and fears in darkness bide.
With every flutter, stories weave,
A tapestry of those who grieve.

In twilight's grasp, the echoes sigh,
As moonlit paths invite a cry.
For in the dark, true hearts do break,
And shadows stir for love's own sake.

They dance on wings of feathered grace,
Tracing the lines of time and space.
A gentle touch from realms apart,
Whispers of life, the beating heart.

Through rustling leaves, the whispers soar,
Where light once gleamed, now shadows pour.
A haunting lullaby awakens dreams,
Of whispered love in silver beams.

Blood-Tinted Stories of the Night

In the depths of night, where silence spills,
Blood-tinted tales evoke deep chills.
Each heartbeat echoes through the dark,
A narrative sealed with a spectral mark.

A raven's call, a somber tune,
Hides the secrets of the moon.
With crimson ink, the stories flow,
Of love and loss, the heart's deep woe.

Ghostly whispers haunt the trees,
With every breeze, a memory flees.
In shadows curled, the stories pulse,
Of passion whether fierce or false.

The night blooms thick with tales untold,
Of warriors brave and hearts so bold.
Their blood runs deep, a legacy grand,
In the midnight air, ghosts make their stand.

Through haunted streets, the visions glide,
In every shadow, dreams abide.
Blood-tinted stories, forever spun,
In the web of night, they have begun.

Sable Wings and Scarlet Stories

In twilight's whisper, secrets unfold,
Where sable wings carry tales untold.
Scarlet stories dance on the breeze,
Enchanting hearts with effortless ease.

Beneath the starry, spellbound sky,
Magic lies where shadows fly.
Each flutter a promise, each breath a dream,
A world woven with silken seam.

Through crystal glades and emerald halls,
The echoes of laughter, the softest calls.
With every flutter, a wish takes flight,
In the embrace of the gentle night.

The moon casts silver on ancient trees,
As time drapes softly, like a warm breeze.
Sable wings flit with tales to share,
Of enchanted realms and treasures rare.

In the hush of dusk, let stories soar,
For magic lives forevermore.
Each scarlet word a treasure stirred,
In the heart of a world where dreams are heard.

Wandering Words on Witching Winds

Wandering words ride the witching winds,
Through the tangled woods where the story begins.
Whispers of magic, soft as a sigh,
Guide the lost souls that wander nearby.

Each note of the breeze, a letter unsealed,
Revealing the secrets that time has concealed.
With each rustle of leaves, a page turns bright,
As shadows and starlight converge in the night.

In corners of dreams, the echoes entwine,
As fate writes its verses on threads of divine.
The heart learns to listen, to feel, to discern,
To dance with the tales that the witching winds churn.

Through valleys of wonder, and peaks draped in lore,
The words weave enchantments that beckon for more.
Perspective shifts like the mist on the shore,
Each twist of a tale opens an unseen door.

So wander with words on this magical breeze,
Let your spirit be light, let your heart feel at ease.
For every adventure begins with a spark,
A whisper of wonder that dances in the dark.

Moonlit Quills and Shadowy Tales

In the quiet of night, when shadows arise,
Moonlit quills trace the dreams in the skies.
With ink that glimmers like starlight's embrace,
A tapestry woven in time and in space.

Each flick of the wrist spins a story anew,
From kingdoms of old to worlds that are blue.
The parchment sighs softly, a canvas alive,
With whispers of magic that dreams can contrive.

Under silver beams, where dreams intertwine,
A whisper of truth in the heart's steady line.
Shadowy tales come alive with each stroke,
As ink spills its secrets, the silence awoke.

With heroes and villains, in battles of fate,
The quill dances swiftly, no time to wait.
Each character breathes life in the night air,
Entwined in a wonder that's fleetingly rare.

So gather your thoughts in moon's tender light,
Let stories unfurl and take graceful flight.
For in the heart's ink, and the quill's gentle sway,
Lies the magic of night, come what may.

The Alchemy of Ink and Feather

In chambers of silence, where shadows conspire,
The alchemy of ink stokes the creative fire.
Feathers of dreams, dipped in twilight's glow,
Guide thoughts to the page where wild wonders flow.

Each letter a potion, each word a spell,
Crafted with care, in a story to tell.
Embers of inspiration burn bright in the night,
As the heart learns to dance in the glow of insight.

With quills like wands, casting letters like charms,
Awakening spirits, igniting their arms.
From the tip of the pen, a universe spins,
In the alchemical dance where creation begins.

Beneath veils of ink, the soul takes flight,
Chasing the shadows, embracing the light.
With each gentle stroke, the world comes alive,
In the wizardry formed where the imagination thrives.

So wield your quill, like a master in tune,
As stories awaken beneath the bright moon.
For in the alchemy of ink and feather,
Lies magic unbound, now and forever.

Crimson Feathers in the Moonlight

In the still of the night, they dance with grace,
Crimson feathers flutter, lost in space.
Beneath the moon's gaze, secrets unfold,
Whispers of magic in stories untold.

Through shadows they weave, a silent flight,
Their beauty enchants in the soft silver light.
Every heartbeat echoes, a spellbinding song,
As the night wraps them gently, where they belong.

With a flick of a wing, the stars align,
Promises glimmer, bright as the divine.
In the depths of the twilight, dreams start to bloom,
Carried by breezes that sweep through the gloom.

Crimson feathers rising, they tease the air,
Painting the night with their mystical flair.
Every shadow a canvas, every glow a brush,
In the tapestry woven, we linger, we hush.

In the heart of the night, their stories ignite,
Crimson feathers whisper, a heart's pure delight.
As dawn breaks the spell, and the night drifts away,
The dreams, like the feathers, in memory stay.

Twilight's Feathered Whispers

In twilight shades, where shadows play,
Feathered whispers beckon, guiding our way.
Softly they soar, through colors and dreams,
Carving the silence with delicate beams.

Each feather a truth, a story to tell,
In the hush of the evening, where wishes dwell.
Underneath the sky, painted in hues,
The night unfurls gently, sharing its views.

With each rustle, secrets drift on the breeze,
Like echoes of laughter through shimmering trees.
The twilight enfolds us, a magical shroud,
As the feathered whispers float soft and proud.

They dance among stars, crafting tales of light,
In the soft velvet of a starry night.
In the heart of the dusk, as dreams intertwine,
Twilight's whispers linger, enchanting, divine.

And as the night deepens, the magic is spun,
In the anthem of dusk, we are all but one.
Feathers take flight, fading into the dark,
While the world holds its breath, waiting for the spark.

Shadowed Plumage and Mystic Dreams

In the realm of shadows, where whispers entwine,
Plumage of midnight, with secrets divine.
Mystic dreams flutter, igniting the night,
Carried on wings bathed in silvery light.

Each feather a portal, to realms far and wide,
A bridge to the unknown, where spirits reside.
Through twilight they glide, with grace and with ease,
As the silence embraces, like a gentle breeze.

With laughter like ripples on a darkened stream,
They beckon us closer, luring with gleam.
In shadows they whisper, weaving their spell,
Where magic is born, and dreamers dwell.

In the heart of the night, beneath starlit skies,
Mystic plumage flickers, a dance that defies.
Held close in our hearts, these dreams gently hum,
As the echoes of night in soft cadence come.

With dawn on the horizon, the shadows take flight,
But in dreams, we remember the thrill of the night.
For among the shadowed plumage, forever we'll roam,
In whispers of magic, we find our true home.

The Enchanted Pen of the Night

In the quiet of darkness, where stories begin,
The enchanted pen flows, weaving tales within.
Each stroke brings to life what dreams dare to say,
As the night whispers secrets in delicate play.

With ink drawn from starlight, and hopes made of fire,
The tales of our hearts become one with desire.
Each word a caress, like the breeze through the trees,
In this sacred moment, every longing can seize.

The enchanted pen dances, on parchment of dreams,
As echoes of laughter float softly on streams.
In the moon's tender gaze, every wish finds its flight,
Scribbling the adventures that glitter in night.

In the hush of creation, where magic holds sway,
The pen traces wonders that wish to convey.
From heart to the paper, like whispers of wings,
The night shares its stories, unveiling all things.

As dawn breaks the spell, and the ink starts to dry,
The tales linger softly as moments float by.
For the enchanted pen weaves a tapestry bright,
Reflecting our souls in the grandeur of night.

The Inked Silence of Night's Quill

In the hush of night's embrace,
Stars whisper secrets to the moon's face.
With each stroke of the quill's might,
Silent stories bloom in twilight.

Shadows dance beneath the trees,
Carrying tales on the gentle breeze.
With ink as dark as the local lore,
Words cascade like a gentle roar.

The pages turn, the silence sings,
In the quiet, magic clings.
Every letter, a mystery spun,
In the rhythm of the night, we run.

A flicker here, a glimpse of fate,
Characters brought to life, innate.
Beneath the watch of the night's eye,
Imagination learns to fly.

So let the ink flow, let it spill,
In every heart, there lies the thrill.
Of worlds unseen and dreams to chase,
Within the inked night's vibrant space.

Fires of Ink and Feathered Flight

Upon the parchment, fires ignite,
In brilliant hues, black and white.
Feathers thrumming with each pen stroke,
Ancient truths in symbols cloak.

The phoenix rises from the ash,
As ink flows like a bright flash.
Words take wing on the breeze of night,
In every tale, the heart takes flight.

Embers glow in the quiet room,
Where thoughts unravel, banish gloom.
Through shadows deep, inspiration's spark,
Guides the way through the silenced dark.

Let whispers weave in soft delight,
As visions shimmer and thoughts take flight.
With dreams adorned in ink and fire,
We craft our fate with endless desire.

So grasp the quill, let passion dwell,
In stories we weave, we cast our spell.
Feathered words, let them ignite,
A journey begun in the heart of night.

A Tapestry Woven in Crimson Hues

Crimson threads in twilight's loom,
Woven tales dispel the gloom.
Each strand whispers of glory lost,
In colors bright, we chart the cost.

Golden suns and silver moons,
Dance in heartbeats, sway in tunes.
Every pattern a heartbeat's sigh,
In the tapestry where dreams rely.

With needle of time, we stitch the seams,
Crafting destinies, chasing dreams.
Through the fabric, shadows play,
Illuminating night and day.

In crimson hues, the stories glow,
A vibrant realm where we shall go.
In stitches strong, our hopes reside,
A tapestry where hearts confide.

So let the art of life unfold,
In woven threads, our journeys told.
Each color sings, a life anew,
In the beauty of crimson's view.

Tales of the Cursed and Feathered Ink

In shadows cast by ancient sin,
The cursed pen begins to spin.
With feathered grace, it tells of woes,
Of hidden truths no one knows.

A sip of ink, a stitch of fate,
In every line, the darkness waits.
Characters trapped in paper chains,
Seeking freedom through their pains.

With every word, the echoes cry,
Of battles fought, of love awry.
The ink spills forth like a river wide,
Carving paths where fears can't hide.

Yet from the depths, new hope shall sprout,
As tales of courage turn about.
From feathered quills with magic laced,
The stories soar, in hearts embraced.

So heed the ink, let courage bind,
In every tale, a way to find.
In cursed shadows and feathered flight,
Lies the strength to conquer night.

Mystical Quills on the Edge of Dusk

In twilight's grasp, the quills take flight,
With whispered tales of ancient night.
They dance upon the parchment bare,
Crafting worlds with tender care.

A flick of ink, a shimmering spark,
Unveils the dreams once held in dark.
Each swish and stroke, a secret told,
Of magic realms and heroes bold.

The stars above begin to gleam,
As shadows wove a gentle dream.
In every curve, a story flows,
A tapestry that subtly glows.

The quills, they sing of lost desire,
Of gallant quests and hearts on fire.
With every line, they softly weave,
A tapestry that none conceive.

So linger here, let silence reign,
In inked embrace, forget your pain.
For on this edge where dusk does fall,
The quills will craft, enchanting all.

Silhouettes of Inked Dreams in the Night

Beneath the moon, the shadows play,
In inked dreams where whispers sway.
The silhouettes of hopes untold,
Awake the magic, bright and bold.

Each stroke a journey into sleep,
Where visions vibrant softly seep.
The pages turn, the stories flow,
Carrying hearts where few may go.

A flicker here, a gentle sigh,
As dreams take shape and begin to fly.
The night unfolds with secrets spun,
In every hue, a tale begun.

In shadows deep, the ink will trace,
The labyrinth of dreams we face.
A canvas vast, where worlds collide,
And life's true magic dares to hide.

So take this moment, let it last,
In silhouettes where time is cast.
For in this night, the dreams ignite,
Their inked glimmer, pure delight.

The Scarlet Plume and the Enchanted Storm

In tempest's roar, the plumage bright,
A scarlet plume, a dazzling sight.
It sails the skies, defying fate,
While magic swirls, it won't abate.

With every gust, the heartstrings pull,
An echoing beat, relentless, full.
The storm it brews, fierce and grand,
Concealing secrets yet unplanned.

As raindrops dance upon the ground,
The plume of crimson spins around.
It twirls and dips, a vibrant flame,
A herald bold of passion's name.

Through thunder's clash and lighting's blink,
The scarlet plume begins to think.
Of journeys vast, of tales untold,
In every storm, brave spirits bold.

Embrace the wild, the storm will call,
Where magic rises, beckoning all.
For in the tempest's heart, we'll find,
The scarlet plume, our dreams entwined.

Whispers of Ink Beneath the Willow

Under the willow, shadows twine,
In whispers soft, the tales align.
The ink flows dark, like rivers deep,
Where secrets hide and memories sleep.

Beneath its boughs, the heart will sigh,
As stories whisper, softly nigh.
With gentle grace, the leaves will sway,
Inviting dreams that drift away.

Each word a petal, drifting down,
Upon the earth, where dreams are sown.
With every stroke, the ink will thread,
A tapestry of life long bled.

The night embraces, quiet and sly,
Beneath the willow's watchful eye.
As time will fold, the ink will weave,
A map of hope, of bliss reprieve.

So linger low, let silence mend,
In whispers soft, let hearts descend.
For in this place, where shadows curl,
The ink will speak, the dreams unfurl.

Scarlet Scribbles Beneath the Boughs

Beneath the trees a secret lies,
In branches high, where shadow sighs.
Scarlet scribbles twist and twine,
Whispered echoes, dreams divine.

A parchment spread on mossy ground,
With fleeting thoughts, a heart unbound.
Nature's ink, in twilight's glow,
Pen strokes wild, the stories flow.

The fireflies dance, a flickering light,
Illuminating words that take flight.
With every stroke, a tale unfolds,
Of ancient woods and treasures untold.

In the dusk, a melody sings,
As the forest weaves with unseen strings.
A tapestry of life and lore,
Underneath the boughs forevermore.

So let the scribbles paint the air,
With colors bright, beyond compare.
For in this realm of whispered dreams,
Scarlet ink forever gleams.

Echoes of a Feathered Muse

Upon the breeze, a feather sways,
In sunlight's dance, it gently plays.
Whispers call from azure skies,
A muse in flight, where magic lies.

The colors shift in twilight's breath,
A story woven through life and death.
With each descent, the whispers soar,
Echoes of tales from ages yore.

A resting place on a silvered branch,
Where dreams of avians take their chance.
Their wings, a brush, as colors blend,
In vibrant hues that never end.

Listen close, for the songs they sing,
Are woven threads of an ancient fling.
With every note, a heart recalls,
The magic that within us calls.

For every flight, a story spun,
Beneath the gaze of a wistful sun.
In echoes soft, the muses tread,
Guiding the paths where dreams are led.

Wrought in Embered Silks

In twilight's glow, the silks arise,
Wrought in embered hues, they surprise.
Threads of fire, spun with grace,
In the loom of time, they find their place.

Dancing shadows on the wall,
Whispered secrets, beck and call.
Fires flicker, tales ignite,
In the velvet of the night.

With every weave, a heart does sigh,
A tapestry beneath the sky.
Silken strands in a swirling dance,
Holding dreams in a fleeting trance.

A cloak of warmth, a shroud of night,
Embered silks absorb the light.
The stories told, in every fold,
Of love, of loss, of courage bold.

So let the fibers intertwine,
In the glow where stars align.
For in the dark, our spirits lift,
Wrought in silks, a precious gift.

The Witch's Ink and Scarlet Veil

In shadows deep, the cauldron stirs,
A witch prepares as night occurs.
With ink of night and scarlet hue,
She conjures spells both old and new.

The paper crinkles with every stroke,
Whispers rise like curling smoke.
The stories dance, both fierce and frail,
Beneath the witch's ink and veil.

With candlelight, the spirit wales,
Through hidden trails and ancient tales.
Each drop a portal, wisdom's kiss,
Calling forth the magic's bliss.

In every line, a path is drawn,
With dreams that linger till the dawn.
Potion facts and fables knit,
Underneath the moon's soft lit.

So find the truths in shadows bold,
As tales of magic start to unfold.
For within the ink, a world lies veiled,
In whispers soft, the heart is hailed.

Incantations on Feathered Lines

In whispers soft, the feathers glide,
Where secrets dwell, and dreams reside.
With moonlit grace, they take their flight,
A dance of magic in the night.

Each fluttered touch, a spell that's cast,
In twilight's glow, the die is cast.
With ink of stars, I pen the fate,
Of winged wonders, we create.

Through ancient woods, where shadows play,
The language flows in wild array.
With every whisper, let hearts unite,
In this enchanted, feathered flight.

The parchment crinkles, tales unfold,
Of mystical creatures, bold and old.
With every verse, the world takes wing,
To feathered lines, our voices sing.

So gather close, and lend your ear,
To tales profound, both far and near.
With every flutter, every rhyme,
In feathered lines, we dance through time.

Tales Not Told in Daylight

In shadows deep, where whispers play,
Tales unfold in a hidden way.
Where creatures roam and secrets hide,
In twilight's arms, that's where we bide.

The moonlight paints the silent scenes,
Of haunted woods and ancient dreams.
With caution, step through veils of night,
For stories thrive where there's no light.

A flicker of fate, a touch of dread,
In every corner, the magic's fed.
The nightingale sings of what's untold,
In shadows' clasp, the brave and bold.

With flickering candles, let voices rise,
To dance and twirl 'neath starry skies.
For only in dark, do truths take flight,
In tales not told in the daylight.

So gather round, and heed the call,
For night shall weave a wondrous thrall.
In hushed tones, let hearts align,
And share the tales of the twilight vine.

The Witch's Script and Velvet Darkness

In velvet darkness, secrets thread,
The witch's script begins to spread.
With swirling ink and candlelight,
She conjures spells to quell the night.

Each booming heart, each whispered name,
In shadows deep, a wild flame.
Her cauldron bubbles with dreams and fears,
The potion brews through silent years.

With shadows dancing, creatures thrum,
To ancient rhythms, they hum and strum.
In velvet darkness, power grows,
As hidden magic spun from woes.

The air grows thick with kindred vibe,
Of tales entwined in mystic tribe.
With every line, a pulse of art,
In witch's script, she plays her part.

So listen well, as night unfolds,
Beyond the stars, the truth beholds.
In velvet darkness, whispers ignite,
The witch's script shall claim the night.

Dancing Shadows and Scarlet Ink

In corners dark, where shadows sway,
A dance begins, both dark and gray.
With scarlet ink, the stories spill,
Of secret lore and hidden will.

The flickering light reveals the shapes,
Of ancient heroes, fates and scrapes.
With every stroke, the tales arise,
In shadows dancing, wisdom lies.

Through rustling leaves and haunted cries,
The memories weave, where silence lies.
In scarlet ink, our hearts will blend,
Through every pain, we shall transcend.

With whispered dreams, the shadows weave,
Of love and loss, we dare believe.
In twilight's grasp, we find our way,
Through dancing shadows, night turns day.

So paint your fears with ink so bold,
In every story, let love unfold.
For under stars, our spirits link,
As we embrace the scarlet ink.

The Witch's Heartbeat Beneath the Ink

In shadows deep, where secrets dwell,
The witch writes magic, casting her spell.
With every stroke, her heartbeat sighs,
And whispers weave through moonlit skies.

Her quill, a wand of ancient lore,
Dances with fate, forevermore.
Ink flows like blood through parchment's vein,
A symphony sung in joy and pain.

Each word a potion, each line a charm,
Binding the night with a tender arm.
Wrapped in the darkness, her truth unfolds,
A tapestry woven with starlit gold.

Beneath the ink, her heartbeat thrums,
Echoing tales of where magic comes.
In every letter, a fragment of soul,
The witch's essence, perfectly whole.

So heed the whispers, oh curious heart,
For the witch's secret is but the start.
Her heartbeat guides, through shadows it sweeps,
In the world of ink, where wonder sleeps.

Ghostly Quills in Twilight's Grasp

When twilight descends with a velvet cloak,
Ghostly quills rise with stories bespoke.
They flutter and dance through the shivering air,
Writing the tales of the forgotten, rare.

With ink from the stars, they pen ancient lore,
Of shadows and whispers, and what lies in store.
Each stroke a beacon, each dot a sigh,
Drawing forth dreams that dare to fly.

Beneath the gaze of a crescent moon,
The quills trace the fate of a lamenting tune.
In solitude's embrace, they softly confine,
The echoes of longing, so sweet, so divine.

In this twilight world, where secrets bleed,
The ghostly quills fulfill every need.
They craft a realm, where spirits roam free,
Blurring the lines of what's you and me.

So linger a moment, let shadows entwine,
With ghostly quills, where magic aligns.
In twilight's tender, unforgettable grasp,
Find tales untold, in a fleeting gasp.

Beneath the Quill of Blood and Ink

In a darkened room, where shadows creep,
The quill of blood awakens from sleep.
It dances on paper, sketching the screams,
Of haunted whispers and shattered dreams.

With every drop of ink, a life is penned,
Tales of betrayal, where heartache won't end.
In crimson stories, secrets unfold,
The ink soaked deep in a heart turned cold.

The witch, a keeper of memories past,
Writes of enchantments that never last.
Under the moon's gaze, her heartbeats sync,
With each word written in blood and ink.

As echoes of laughter turn into moans,
The quill makes magic from heart's very bones.
Through veils of sorrow, it weaves and twirls,
A testament born of the witching worlds.

So beware the tales that bleed and bind,
For beneath the quill lies a fate enshrined.
In blood and ink, the stories relate,
A haunting symphony of love and fate.

Scarlets in the Witching Hour

In the witching hour, when shadows fall,
Scarlets bloom bright, enchanting all.
With petals of velvet, they catch the sight,
Whispers of magic linger in the night.

The witch twirls within her garden's grace,
Each scarlet flower a warm embrace.
They dance with the wind, creating a sway,
In a perfumed trance, they beckon and play.

Beneath the stars, where secrets are spun,
The scarlet blooms pulse with the moon and sun.
Every petal a wish, every fragrance a plea,
In the heart of the night, wild and free.

With roots in the earth, they drink up the dreams,
Of moonlit stories and silver screams.
Amongst the shadows, they thrive and bloom,
Casting out darkness, reviving the room.

So when the clock strikes, and stillness reigns,
Look for the scarlets where magic remains.
For in the witching hour, they sing their tune,
An ode to the night, under the watchful moon.

The Twilight Quill and Secrets of the Arcane

In twilight's glow, where whispers dwell,
A quill does weave its mystic spell.
With every stroke, a tale is spun,
Of ancient texts and battles won.

Beneath the stars, the shadows creep,
Guarding secrets that silence keep.
The ink flows dark, a river's song,
As memories swirl, both fierce and strong.

In hidden nooks, the pages sigh,
A longing glance, where dreams can fly.
Each word a spark of magic bright,
A bridge between the day and night.

With fleeting thoughts on parchment laid,
The wizard's lore shall never fade.
A quill in hand, the bold shall soar,
To realms uncharted, evermore.

Though dangers lurk in shadows' grasp,
The heart of courage, we must clasp.
For secrets learned and power gained,
In twilight's hour, let none be feigned.

Rose-Tipped Words Dancing with Shadows

A rose-tipped quill in hand, I write,
Words like petals, soft and light.
They dance with shadows, flicker bright,
In the quiet of a moonlit night.

Each syllable a fragrant bloom,
Dispelling echoes of the gloom.
With every stroke, my spirit twirls,
In whispers shared, the magic unfurls.

The ink is drawn from dreams that fade,
Painting visions in the glade.
The shadows sway, a waltz divine,
In tales of old, our fates entwine.

A symphony of hearts that bind,
In words by twilight's grace defined.
The rose-tipped quill, it glows anew,
In secrets kept and promises true.

So let us dance in ink and light,
With shadows as our guiding rite.
For in this world of dreams and schemes,
The heart finds solace in whispered dreams.

The Witch's Palette and the Ink of Fate

A witch's palette, hues so rare,
With strokes that weave through midnight air.
Each color holds a tale untold,
Of passion, loss, and fortunes bold.

In twilight's brush, the night does blend,
Creating echoes that never end.
The ink of fate, both dark and bright,
Reveals the paths of wrong and right.

With each mix, a potion brews,
An artful dance of reds and blues.
From emerald greens to twilight gold,
The visions captured, brave and bold.

A palette spread upon the floor,
The sorceress beckons to explore.
For every shade and hue she paints,
A story blooms, where magic faints.

In vibrant strokes, the world awakes,
To weave the dreams that passion makes.
The witch's heart, an open gate,
With every stroke, she meets her fate.

Secrets Scribbled in the Twilight's Embrace

In twilight's embrace, secrets lie,
Like whispered dreams that softly sigh.
Each page a canvas, words take flight,
Illuminated by the fading light.

With ink that glimmers, bound in fate,
The shadows weave a dance of late.
Scribbled truths that pull my heart,
In twilight's arms, they fall apart.

The quill moves swift, with fervent breath,
In every stroke, there lies a death.
Yet from the ashes, life begins,
A cycle set where hope still spins.

What once was lost, now finds its place,
In the tender warmth of night's embrace.
Each secret penned, a path revealed,
In twilight's shroud, our fates are sealed.

So gather 'round and read the scrolls,
For in the ink are seeking souls.
Together forged, let courage rise,
In the twilight's hue, our spirits fly.

The Sorceress's Plumage in the Twilight

In twilight's glow, a sorceress twirls,
Her plumage soft, in shades of pearls.
With whispers sweet, enchantments weave,
In shadows deep, her dreams believe.

The stars align, a dance so bright,
Her laughter echoes through the night.
A tapestry of magic spun,
The moonlit path has just begun.

With every flutter, secrets sing,
As night unfolds, the shadows cling.
Her feathers brush against the air,
A mystic call, beyond compare.

Through forest dark, her spirit glides,
A guardian where the magic bides.
With each soft call, the fireflies shine,
In twilight's arms, her heart entwined.

Inkblots on a Witch's Hearth

Beside the flames, a kettle hums,
Inkblots dance, as magic drums.
With quill in hand, the witch will write,
Her stories twirling, day to night.

Each stroke a spell, each line a dream,
In swirling smoke, her thoughts may gleam.
A hearth ablaze with tales untold,
In shadows deep, the secrets unfold.

Potions simmer, colors bright,
Crafting potions in the fading light.
Her ink a river, flowing bold,
A canvas wide, where legends grow old.

The moon observes with pale delight,
As inkblots dance in the soft twilight.
The witch, she knows, her heart afire,
With every line, she builds desire.

The Gloomy Quill and the Secrets of the Stars

A gloomy quill with ink of night,
Records the secrets, beyond our sight.
Beneath the eaves, in shadows cast,
The stars above are boundless, vast.

Each stroke reveals the hidden lore,
Of cosmic truths, and tales of yore.
In silence deep, the whispers trace,
The tales of worlds, in time and space.

The quill it dances, swift and sure,
With ideas bright, yet spirits pure.
Each letter penned a wishful sigh,
As starlit dreams begin to fly.

In darkened corners, wisdom gleams,
The secrets woven in silver beams.
With every turn, the heavens sigh,
As the quill composes lullabies.

Raven Wings Marking the Midnight Sky

Raven wings in midnight's glow,
Across the heavens, wild winds blow.
With ancient calls, they pierce the air,
Marking the sky where dreams repair.

Each feather dark, a tale to tell,
Of shadows deep and morning's bell.
In flight they weave a tapestry,
Of secrets held in mystery.

The moonlight glimmers on their flight,
Guiding lost souls through the night.
With whispered spells, they rule the dark,
In each soft flap, an endless spark.

Beneath their wings, adventure calls,
In echoes loud, in distant halls.
Through midnight's veil, they sweep and soar,
Raven wings, forevermore.

Blood-Red Wings Against the Dark Sky

In the night where shadows creep,
A figure takes to muted flight.
Crimson feathers cut the gloom,
Wings spread wide, they pierce the night.

A siren song of distant wails,
Echoes through the haunted trees.
The darkness starts to unveil,
As fear submits to a chilling breeze.

With a gaze as fierce as flame,
They glide past whispers of despair.
Each heartbeat pulses the same,
A promise hidden in the air.

Over sleeping towns below,
They spread their wings, a fierce embrace.
With every glide, new tales grow,
A tapestry that time can't erase.

Veils of night, entwined with light,
In the dance of dusk and dawn.
Blood-red wings take to their flight,
In a world where hope is reborn.

Mystic Pens and Feathered Shadows

In a realm where ink flows free,
And thoughts take shape in ghostly trails.
Mystic pens carve destiny,
While feathered shadows weave their tales.

Every stroke ignites a spark,
In whispers that the pages hold.
With every line, we mark the dark,
Impressions of a dream retold.

Those shadows dance, they flutter near,
A tapestry of thought and flight.
They guide the hand when pen meets ear,
Crafting visions in the night.

Across the parchment, echoes sing,
Of battles bold and timeless charms.
Mystic tales with blessings bring,
As inspiration's spell disarms.

So let your thoughts take wing and soar,
With pens that breathe life into dreams.
Feathered shadows at your door,
Whispering softly, or so it seems.

Secrets Inked in Crimson Hues

Beneath the moon's soft, watchful eye,
Secrets linger in the dark.
Crimson ink, a silent cry,
Unfolds stories, leaves its mark.

Every page, a tale embraced,
Of hearts entwined and hopes betrayed.
Ciphers in the lines are traced,
In whispered truths, the fears displayed.

They speak of love and loss combined,
A tapestry of pain and grace.
In every word, a soul resigned,
Longing for a warm embrace.

The pen, a vessel of our fate,
With crimson hues, it writes the night.
In secrets inked, we contemplate,
The labyrinth of wrong and right.

As dawn approaches, shadows wane,
And in the light, our truth shines bright.
Crimson tales, born of the pain,
Will weave new dreams in morning light.

The Enigma of Twilight Feathers

Once twilight falls, the magic stirs,
In feathers cloaked, the spirits play.
An enigma shrouded, soft murmurs,
Guide the lost, then fade away.

With wings of dusk, they slip through time,
A mystery in every glide.
The beauty hidden in the rhyme,
In shadows where their secrets bide.

Each feather holds a tale to tell,
Of midnight whispers, sweet and sly.
In twilight's glow, they weave a spell,
As dreams take flight and softly sigh.

From ancient woods to vast, still skies,
They dance on breezes, light and free.
An artful grace in their demise,
The enigma wrought in reverie.

So let the twilight's magic weave,
An understanding deep and wide.
In feathered dreams, we must believe,
For in the dark, our hopes abide.

The Basilisk's Feathered Pen

In depths of stone, the whispers sigh,
A feathered pen, secrets entwined,
Ink like shadows, the pages cry,
Truths and tales, in darkness defined.

With scales of emerald, it glides with grace,
Charmed by the magic, it weaves the night,
Words like spells in a hidden place,
Crafting legends, in dim candlelight.

In ancient tomes where echoes dwell,
The basilisk's gaze unveils the past,
Each stroke of ink, a whispered spell,
Unlocking stories forever cast.

Feathered hopes on parchment soar,
Chronicles born from twilight's breath,
In every tale, a lore of yore,
Binding life, entwined with death.

So pen your dreams with daring flair,
Let magic dance on every line,
In the basilisk's secrets, find your care,
For in each word, your heart will shine.

Nightfall's Ink and Feathered Light

As dusk descends, the world turns still,
Night whispers softly, the stars awake,
Feathers fall gently, like dreams they spill,
Drawing the night with every stroke they make.

Ink of shadows, mysteries near,
Sketching the tales of the moon's embrace,
Every flicker, a stitch in fear,
While dreams dance lightly, a silken trace.

The creatures stir in the silver light,
Tales woven in the air so fine,
Ink spills warmth in the dimming night,
Scripted stories in a cosmic line.

With feathered quills, we find our voice,
Through the swirling ink, we weave our fate,
Embracing shadows, we make our choice,
In the glow of night, we celebrate.

For in the stillness, the heart takes flight,
Every word a lantern, bright and true,
In the dark of night, with ink and light,
We forge our tales, in skies of blue.

Secrets Written in Ember's Embrace

In flickering flames, the secrets hide,
Embers whisper, a soft-lit dance,
Stories of old on the coals reside,
Captured in amber, a timeless trance.

With every spark, a memory flies,
Filling the air with tales untold,
The heat of the night, a gentle sighs,
Turning the mundane into the gold.

Through twilight's breath, the shadows play,
Sketching moments in gentle glow,
In ember's embrace, fears melt away,
As firelight paints the tales we know.

So gather 'round where the warm flame gleams,
Let voices intertwine in golden light,
The stories mingle with all our dreams,
In ember's embrace, we ignite the night.

For every flicker holds a desire,
Whispers of hope in the smoky air,
Under the stars, we build our fire,
In secrets shared, we are laid bare.

Stories Unspooled Beneath the Stars

Beneath the stars, the night unfolds,
Threads of silver weave stories bright,
Each twinkling point, a mystery holds,
Waiting for hearts to take flight.

With whispers sweet, the cosmos sings,
Stories told in celestial glow,
In the tapestry of time, it brings,
A woven path, where dreams flow.

From constellations, old tales arise,
Casting light on the hidden past,
With every gaze, a world complies,
Unspooling memories, vast and vast.

So let your spirit roam the skies,
And dance with echoes of ages gone,
For in the night, the universe lies,
Weaving threads of fate, till the dawn.

With every heartbeat, the stories blend,
Beneath the stars where our hopes reside,
In the night's embrace, we forever mend,
For tales unspooled will never hide.